30 Under 300

healthy, unique recipes under 300 calories

Kimberly Capella

acknowledgements

This book is so much more than just me. Thanks to everyone in the social media community involved in this book during its creation process; your contributions and desires are very much appreciated. Jess Ker, a contest winner, deserves recipe credits for the final recipe in this book. I need to thank all of my supporters through these past few years that have encouraged me when I couldn't encourage myself enough. Your belief in me truly drives me to keep creating content for the world. This cookbook would also be nothing without Tom Morkes and his publishing wisdom. Thanks so much Tom for the constant feedback, communication, and guidance towards making a great cookbook for the world. Again, your belief in my work and push for its success is empowering. Icons included were made from www.flaticon.com by Freepik.

contents

dairy free
gluten free
vegan
paleo

*"sometimes the smallest step in the right direction
ends up being the biggest step of your life. tip toe
if you must, but take the step."*

introduction

First of all, thank you! Welcome to the world of healthy and delicious indulgence. This is the third cookbook of mine and by FAR my favorite. You'll find that it is so much more than a healthy-eating cookbook. Beyond sugar-free, guilt-free and low calorie treats, I want to ensure this book conveys a message of total mental and physical health. It's easy to get wrapped up in the vanity aspect of healthy eating; it's important to take time to work on mental well-being as well. As you browse this book and find your favorite recipes that cater to your specific dietary needs, pause and reflect on other aspects of your life that will get you to where you want to be. I really hope you enjoy.

kitchen staples

I kept these recipes as simple yet flavorful as possible, using common ingredients that anyone can get in stores or online. The internet is a powerful place. Here are the most important baking basics to have, plus my personal favorites.

pantry

Old-fashioned rolled oats (or instant)
Almond meal/flour
Coconut flour
Peanut flour
Whey protein powder (vanilla, chocolate)
Ground flaxseed
Stevia (bagged baking stevia and packets)
Sugar free chocolate chips and/or cacao nibs
Sugar free pudding mix
Unsweetened cocoa powder
Unsweetened shredded coconut
Nut butters (almond, cashew, peanut, etc.)
Coconut oil
Canned coconut milk
Canned pumpkin puree
Canned chickpeas
Nuts
Dates
Raisins
Cinnamon
Baking powder
Baking soda
Vanilla extract
Nonstick cooking spray

refrigerator & freezer

Fresh fruit
Frozen berries
Eggs
Unsweetened applesauce
Unsweetened almond milk
Sugar free maple syrup (also called breakfast syrup, found with traditional pancake syrups)
Sugar free jelly

baking tips & hacks

There are a lot of tricks to baking, whether it be understanding how certain flours work, how to make recipes fluffy, what difference temperature makes, what can be substituted with what...I could go on forever. I want to make things as easy as I can. So let's go through the hacks together.

1. Baking stevia and stevia packets are different. Packets are concentrated and are good to use for single-serve recipes. Bagged baking stevia is more mild of a sweetness, so it's good to use as a sugar substitute in baking multiple-serving recipes. If a recipe calls for baking stevia, you do not want to use the equivalent of that in stevia packets.

2. Anytime stevia is used, you can of course use any sweetener you prefer instead. That includes, coconut sugar, date sugar, honey, maple syrup, or whatever floats your boat. But you'll find that this cookbook focuses on stevia to sweeten as a low calorie, all natural option. When sugar free maple syrup is used, regular maple syrup works equally.

3. Moistening agents can all be substituted for one another. Examples of moistening agents: canned pumpkin puree, unsweetened applesauce, mashed banana, greek yogurt. They are all interchangeable exactly.

4. Grinding oats vs. store-bought oat flour. Yes, there is a difference between measuring oats then grinding it down and just measuring oat flour from a bag. But that difference is insignificant. It's not enough of a difference to make a huge deal about it. So if I use a half cup of oats and grind it down, you can use a half cup of store-bought oat flour. It's cheaper to grind your own.

5. Defining the flours. Almond flour is moist and makes recipes dense. Coconut flour absorbs liquid with super ultra-powers; it makes recipes light, fluffy, and cakey. Oats are a pretty standard base flour to use in any recipe; oat flour can be substituted with other "standard" flours such as buckwheat, spelt, whole wheat, all-purpose, etc.

6. For all gluten free recipes, be sure you are using gluten-free certified oats. If spelt flour (not gluten free) is used, you can substitute it with buckwheat flour.

7. If you want your recipe to rise & be fluffy while baking, don't forget the baking powder. I'll just leave it at that.

8. Oils can all be substituted for one another. So coconut oil can be substituted with any preferred oil, but it won't be as sweet since coconut adds a touch of subtle sweet. Alternatively, unsweetened applesauce can sometimes be used instead of coconut oil for a low-fat option. Of course, this isn't true for every recipe, but it's a safe bet for most recipes.

9. I use dates a lot. It's a sweet, simple ingredient. Make sure to find the freshest, best dates. If you don't, you'll be stuck with firm, old dates that are difficult to blend or taste. If you can only find firm dates, soak them in water overnight before blending them for a recipe.

10. Whey protein is a good binding agent, but can make recipes like brick if used in excess. Never have whey protein make up more than half of your recipe ingredients or you will regret it; otherwise, it creates a nice light cakey texture. If you don't have whey protein or can't have it (it is a milk derivative), most of the recipes in this book are okay without any at all. Best alternative choices: egg protein, pea protein, rice protein, or any name brand plant-based protein powder mixture.

11. A typical scoop of protein powder is 28-30 g. So for reference, when a recipe in this book calls for 1/2 scoop, it needs 15 g. For a recipe needing 1 whole scoop, use 30 g.

12. If you are dairy free and/or vegan, I use chocolate chips in a lot of my recipes. It is fairly easy to find milk free chocolate, actually! Look at dark chocolate options since it usually does not contain any milk.

13. If you can't have eggs, you can make a flax egg instead. 1 flax egg is 1 TBSP ground flaxseed mixed with 2.5 TBSP warm water. Let it sit 5 minutes to thicken before using. This is used in place of 1 whole egg or 2 egg whites.

14. Invest in a food scale. It helps so much to double-check your volume

measurements, especially since baking can be so particular sometimes.

15. Know these conversions! For anything not listed, there are easy-to-use conversion calculators free online.

1 oz = 28 g
16 oz = 1 lb
1 TBSP = 3 tsp
1/2 TBSP = 1.5 tsp
4 TBSP = 1/4 cup
16 TBSP = 1 cup
1 tsp = 5 ml
1 TBSP = 15 ml
350° F = 180° C

16. Best way to know when a baked recipe is done – stick a toothpick in it! If the toothpick comes out of the food with anything on it, it's not done baking. If the toothpick comes out clean, it's done.

"almost every successful person begins with two beliefs: the future can be better than the present, and I have the power to make it so."

under 5 ingredients

The easiest recipes around. Nothing crazy or complicated in this chapter. No wizardry or rocket science or 360 flips while juggling fire on a unicycle. Just simple recipes sure to succeed in every way.

Apple Pie Cookie Bites

1 cup walnuts (or almonds)
1 cup dried apple slices (1 oz)
1/2 cup pitted dates (80 g)
1/4 tsp apple pie spice
1 tsp vanilla extract

Place the walnuts in a food processor and blend until a grainy flour forms. Add the remaining ingredients and blend again. While it is blending, scrape the sides down until everything forms a thick paste. Use a heaping teaspoon to individually mold the paste into 20 balls.

serves 4

nutritional information per serving
275 calories; 18 g fat, 26 g carbs (4 g fiber), 5 g protein

dairy free, gluten free, vegan, paleo

No Bake Whipped Peanut Butter Pie

Crust
1/2 cup pitted dates (80 g)
1/4 cup raw oats (20 g)
2 TBSP unsweetened shredded coconut

Filling
1 can full fat coconut milk, chilled
1/4 cup peanut butter

In a food processor or small blender, blend all of the crust ingredients. If needed, add 2-3 TBSP water to help blend everything. It should be a moldable paste rather than grainy. Press the crust along the base of a mini pie dish. Then, open the can of coconut milk. You want to chill the can first so the layers separate. Pour off the thin, liquid layer and just keep the thick white layer. Whip the coconut milk with the peanut butter. Pour this on top of the crust. Then freeze the pie for 1.5-2 hours. Cut into 6 slices, then serve chilled.

serves 6

nutritional information per serving
250 calories; 25 g fat, 17 g carbs (2 g fiber), 4 g protein

dairy free, gluten free, vegan

Toasted Pecan Ice Cream

1 can full fat coconut milk, chilled
1/3 cup baking stevia
1 tsp vanilla extract
1/3 cup chopped pecans
1/2 tsp cinnamon

Toss together your chopped pecans and cinnamon in a small bowl. Spread out on a baking tray and bake at 350⁰ F for 5 minutes until lightly toasted. In a food processor, blend the coconut milk, stevia, and vanilla extract. Be sure to chill the can of coconut milk before using so the layers separate. Pour off the thin, liquid layer and just keep the thick white layer to use. Mix in the toasted pecans. Place everything in a sealed container and freeze for 3-4 hours, mixing frequently to make it extra creamy.

serves 4

nutritional information per serving
242 calories; 34 g fat, 5 g carbs (1 g fiber), 3 g protein

dairy free, gluten free, vegan, paleo

Coffee Cream Bars

1 cup pitted dates (160 g)
1/2 cup raw oats
1/4 cup water
4 frozen bananas (approx. 440 g)
1 TBSP + 1 tsp instant coffee powder
2 oz sugar free chocolate

In a food processor, blend together the pitted dates, raw oats, and water. Be sure to use soft dates; if your dates are too firm, soak them in water for at least 3 hours before blending. Line a 9x9 dish with saran wrap; this will be helpful later to remove the bars. Press the blended mixture along the inside of the 9x9 dish to create a solid base. Then, place the frozen bananas and instant coffee into the food processor. This may take 3-5 minutes to fully blend the bananas; be patient. Once a thick coffee cream is visible, evenly spread it on top of the base layer previously placed in the 9x9 dish. Melt 2 oz of sugar free chocolate and drizzle it on top of the coffee cream layer. Freeze for 2 hours or more, then slice into 8 pieces and serve. Store any extra servings in the freezer.

To ensure this recipe is dairy free and vegan, use dark chocolate (no milk).

serves 8

nutritional information per serving
163 calories; 3 g fat, 32 g carbs (3 g fiber), 2 g protein

dairy free, gluten free, vegan

Single Serve Cinnamon Roll

Dough
1/3 cup oats
2 TBSP unsweetened applesauce
1 TBSP coconut oil
1/4 tsp baking powder
1 stevia packet

Inside
1/8 tsp cinnamon
1/8 tsp stevia

Grind the oats into a flour. Add the remaining dough ingredients and mix evenly. Roll the dough out flat onto parchment paper; it should be about 1-1.5 inch wide and 1/2 inch thick. Mix your cinnamon and stevia; sift it evenly on top of the dough. Then, roll the dough into a spiral cinnamon roll. Place into a small ramekin or mug, then microwave for 1.5 minutes. Enjoy.

Suggested toppings: sugar free maple syrup; cinnamon protein powder mixed with water.

serves 1

nutritional information per serving
233 calories; 16 g fat, 21 g carbs (3 g fiber), 3 g protein

dairy free, gluten free, vegan

"never allow waiting to become a habit. live your dreams and take risks. life is happening now."

“there is nothing more dangerous in life than comfort.”

under 5 minutes

Recipes here can all be made in under five minutes – because ain't nobody got time for that. Okay some people do. And I guess it really depends on the day. And mood... Regardless, these are some great, quick recipes to have hidden up your sleeve on hectic days.

Snickers Parfait

1.5 oz silken tofu
1 TBSP peanut butter
1 stevia packet
1/4 cup pitted dates (40 g)
1/2 TBSP unsweetened cocoa powder
1.5 TBSP water
1 TBSP chopped peanuts

With a small blender or hand blender, puree the silken tofu, peanut butter, and stevia until smooth and creamy. Set to the side. Then, blend the dates, cocoa powder, and water. If you have trouble blending this together, add a little water until it forms a thick mixture. Layer the two blended mixtures in a cup and top with chopped peanuts. Enjoy.

If you prefer, the tofu can be substituted with greek yogurt, but it will no longer be dairy free and vegan.

serves 1

nutritional information per serving
295 calories; 13 g fat, 36 g carbs (6 g fiber), 8 g protein

dairy free, gluten free, vegan

Maple Pecan French Toast Mugcake

2 egg whites
2 TBSP unsweetened almond milk
2 TBSP sugar free maple syrup
1 stevia packet
1/2 tsp vanilla extract
2 slices bread of choice
1 TBSP chopped pecans

Mix the egg whites, almond milk, syrup, stevia, and vanilla extract. Then, cut the bread into small cubes and soak it in the egg mixture for 1 minute. Once the bread has absorbed the egg mixture, stir in the chopped pecans. Spray a mug with nonstick spray and pour the entire bread mixture in. Microwave for 2 minutes. Let cool, then enjoy.

For the bread, 40 calorie per slice light bread is preferred. Not only does it cut calories, but it tends to soak up the egg mixture great for cooking. If gluten free, be sure to use gluten free bread.

serves 1

nutritional information per serving
178 calories; 6 g fat, 21 g carbs (7 g fiber), 18 g protein

dairy free, gluten free friendly

White Chocolate Pistachio Mugcake

1/3 cup raw oats
2 tsp sugar free pistachio pudding mix
1/2 scoop vanilla whey protein powder
1 egg white
2 TBSP unsweetened almond milk
1/2 tsp baking powder
1 stevia packet
2 TBSP sugar free white chocolate chips

First, grind the oats into a flour. Then in a bowl, mix the oat flour with the remaining ingredients. Pour the batter in a mug sprayed with nonstick spray. Microwave for 1 minute. Let cool for 1-2 minutes, then flip onto a plate and enjoy.

If dairy free, omit the whey protein and substitute white chocolate with dark chocolate.

serves 1

nutritional information per serving
265 calories; 8 g fat, 30 g carbs (3 g fiber), 20 g protein

dairy free friendly, gluten free

PB&J Fudge

1/2 cup chickpeas, cooked, rinsed, and drained
1/4 cup peanut flour
1/4 cup melted coconut oil
2 stevia packets
1/4 cup peanut butter
1/3 cup sugar free maple syrup
1/4 cup sugar free strawberry jelly

In a small blender or food processor, blend everything up except for the jelly. Line an 8x8 dish with cling wrap (for easy removal later) and pour in the fudge batter. Dollop the jelly into the batter and lightly swirl. Freeze for 1.5-2 hours. Cut into 16 pieces and enjoy. Store any extras in the refrigerator.

serves 16

nutritional information per serving
73 calories; 6 g fat, 4 g carbs (1 g fiber), 2 g protein

dairy free, gluten free, vegan

Single Serve Microwave Chocolate Chip Cookie

2 TBSP buckwheat flour
1 TBSP almond flour/meal
1 TBSP peanut butter
1 TBSP water
1 egg yolk
1 stevia packet
1 TBSP sugar free chocolate chips

Mix together all of the ingredients in a small bowl. Place the dough on a plate and microwave for 1.5 minutes. Let cool and enjoy.

Oat flour could be used instead of buckwheat flour.

serves 1

nutritional information per serving
298 calories; 20 g fat, 20 g carbs (4 g fiber), 10 g protein

dairy free, gluten free

"get out of your own way. stop the paralysis by analysis. dream your dream, then wake up and bring it to life."

Dr. Steve Maraboli

"in the end, they that make no mistakes make nothing at all."

cookies

Cookies! Sweet, sweet cookies. The dessert of all desserts. Cookies cover all the bases: crispy for the crunch-lover, soft for the comfort seeker, stuffed for those that love surprises. Who doesn't love cookies?! Don't actually answer that.

Peanut Butter Stuffed Pumpkin Cookies

2/3 cup raw oats
1/4 cup almond meal/flour
1/2 scoop vanilla whey protein powder
1/4 cup baking stevia
1/2 tsp baking powder
1/2 tsp pumpkin spice
1/4 cup canned pumpkin puree
1 egg white
2 TBSP melted coconut oil
1 TBSP + 2 tsp peanut butter

Preheat the oven to 350⁰ F. Grind the oats into a flour. In a medium bowl, add the remaining ingredients except for the peanut butter. Continue to mix until a thick cookie dough forms. Once evenly mixed, roll the batter into 10 cookie dough balls, placing each on a baking sheet sprayed with nonstick spray. In the center of each dough ball, place ½ tsp of peanut butter, completely covering the peanut butter with the cookie dough. Lightly flatten each cookie on the sheet, then bake at 350⁰ F for 12 minutes. Remove, let cool 5 minutes, and enjoy.

If dairy free, whey protein can be omitted entirely.

serves 10

nutritional information per serving
88 calories; 6 g fat, 5 g carbs (1 g fiber), 4 g protein

dairy free friendly, gluten free

Almond Butter Thumbprint Cookies

1 cup raw oats
1/4 cup baking stevia
1/4 cup almond meal/flour
2 TBSP unsweetened almond milk
1 whole egg
1/4 cup almond butter
1/4 tsp baking soda
10 TBSP sugar free raspberry jelly

Preheat the oven to 350° F. Grind the oats into a flour. Then add the remaining ingredients except for the jelly and mix evenly. Spray a baking tray with nonstick spray, then dollop the batter onto the tray to create 10 cookies. Indent each cookie slightly with the back of a spoon. Bake at 350° F for 8-9 minutes. Let cool for 10 minutes, then dollop 1 TBSP sugar free jelly on the top of each cookie.

serves 10

nutritional information per serving
102 calories; 6 g fat, 12 g carbs (4 g fiber), 4 g protein

dairy free, gluten free

Sticky Caramel Cookies

3/4 cup almond meal/flour
1 scoop vanilla whey protein powder
1 tsp baking soda
pinch of salt
3/4 cup pitted dates (120 g)
1 TBSP coconut oil
2 TBSP water

Preheat the oven to 350⁰ F. Grind the dates in a blender to chop them up finely; use fresh dates or soak them in water for 3 hours first. Once chopped, blend the dates with the remaining ingredients. Spray a baking sheet with nonstick spray. Dollop the batter onto the sheet to form 5 cookies. Bake at 350⁰ F for 8 minutes. Let cool, then eat.

These cookies are particularly good when served cold. If dairy free, whey protein can be omitted entirely.

serves 5

nutritional information per serving
214 calories; 1 g fat, 22 g carbs (4 g fiber), 9 g protein

dairy free friendly, gluten free

White Chocolate Raspberry Cookies

1/2 cup coconut flour
1/4 cup baking stevia
3/4 cup fresh raspberries
1 tsp baking soda
1/4 cup unsweetened almond milk
1/3 cup cashew butter
1 whole egg
1 egg white
1 oz sugar free white chocolate chips

Preheat the oven to 350⁰ F. Mix everything in a bowl. Form the dough into 7 thick cookies, lightly flattening each on a baking sheet sprayed with nonstick spray. Bake at 350⁰ F for 10-12 minutes until lightly browned.

If dairy free or paleo, use dark chocolate (no milk) or omit the chocolate entirely.

serves 7

nutritional information per serving
150 calories; 10 g fat, 12 g carbs (4 g fiber), 5 g protein

dairy free friendly, gluten free, paleo friendly

Cookie Dough Bars

3/4 cup raw oats
1/4 cup coconut flour
1/4 cup unsweetened applesauce
1/4 cup coconut oil
1/3 cup almond milk
1/2 tsp vanilla extract
1 stevia packet
1 oz sugar free dark chocolate chips + 1/2 oz for topping

Grind the oats into a flour. Then add it to the remaining ingredients (except ½ oz chocolate) into a medium bowl and mix. Once even, spread your batter into an 8x8 dish lined with cling wrap (for easy removal later). Melt the remaining 1/2 oz dark chocolate and drizzle on top. Place your dish in the refrigerator to set for 1 hour. Once firm, slice into 8 pieces and enjoy. Store any extras in the refrigerator.

serves 8

nutritional information per serving
139 calories; 10 g fat, 12 g carbs (3 g fiber), 2 g protein

dairy free, gluten free, vegan

“being afraid of things going wrong isn’t the way to make things go right.”

muffins

Ever watch muffins rise? Okay good don't, because it gets boring. I know from experience. My point is – the end result is amazing. A soft, fluffy treat that's almost a cake but...not. Muffins deserve their own chapter.

Peanut Butter Banana Muffins

3 ripe bananas
1 whole egg
1/4 cup peanut butter
1 tsp baking powder
1.25 cups raw instant oats
1/4 cup almond meal/flour
1/2 tsp vanilla extract

Preheat the oven to 350⁰ F. In a bowl, mash the bananas as much as you can. Then, add the egg, peanut butter, and vanilla extract. Mix evenly. Add the remaining ingredients and mix well. Once evenly mixed, spray a cupcake tray with nonstick spray. Disperse your batter into 9 cupcake molds. Bake at 350⁰ F for 18 minutes. Enjoy.

serves 9

nutritional information per serving
151 calories; 6 g fat, 20 g carbs (3 g fiber), 5 g protein

dairy free, gluten free

Blackberry Crisp Muffins

1/2 cup raw oats
2 TBSP almond meal/flour
1 TBSP coconut flour
1 egg white
1/4 cup unsweetened almond milk
2 stevia packets
1/2 tsp baking powder
1/4 cup fresh blackberries
2 TBSP granola (for topping)

Preheat the oven to 350° F. Grind the oats into a flour. Then add the remaining ingredients in a bowl (except for the granola) and mix evenly. Spray a cupcake tray with nonstick spray, and pour your batter into two cupcake molds. Sprinkle the granola on top of the muffins. Bake at 350° F for 18-20 minutes. Enjoy.

If gluten free, ensure your granola is gluten free certified.

serves 2

nutritional information per serving
187 calories; 7 g fat, 25 g carbs (6 g fiber), 9 g protein

dairy free, gluten free

Almond Joy Muffins

3/4 cup raw oats
1/4 cup almond meal/flour
2 egg whites
2 TBSP almond butter
1/4 cup unsweetened almond milk
1/4 cup baking stevia
1 tsp baking powder
1/3 cup unsweetened shredded coconut
1/4 cup sugar free chocolate chips
1 TBSP sliced almonds

Preheat the oven to 350⁰ F. In a blender, grind the oats into a flour. Then add the remaining ingredients except for the shredded coconut, chocolate chips, and sliced almonds. Blend again. Once blended, stir in the shredded coconut and chocolate chips until even. Spray a cupcake pan with nonstick spray and pour the batter into 4 cupcake molds. Sprinkle the tops with sliced almonds. Bake at 350⁰ F for 15 minutes. Remove, let cool for 5-7 minutes, then enjoy.

If dairy free, use dark chocolate (no milk).

serves 4

nutritional information per serving
286 calories; 20 g fat, 25 g carbs (5 g fiber), 9 g protein

dairy free, gluten free

Lemon Poppyseed Muffins

1/2 cup raw oats
1/2 scoop vanilla whey protein powder
1 TBSP coconut flour
1 egg white
2 TBSP water
1 TBSP + 1 tsp lemon juice
1/2 tsp lemon zest
2 stevia packets
1/2 tsp baking powder
1/4 tsp almond extract
1/2 tsp poppy seeds

Preheat the oven to 350^0 F. Grind the oats into a flour. Then add it to the remaining ingredients in a bowl and mix evenly. Spray a cupcake mold with nonstick spray and pour your batter into two cupcake molds. Bake at 350^0 F for 20 minutes. Enjoy.

If dairy free, omit the protein powder entirely.

serves 2

nutritional information per serving
135 calories; 3 g fat, 18 g carbs (4 g fiber), 12 g protein

dairy free friendly, gluten free

Chocolate Pistachio Muffins

1/2 cup raw oats
1/2 cup almond meal/flour
1/2 cup baking stevia
1/2 cup canned pumpkin puree
1/2 cup unsweetened almond milk
1/4 cup unsweetened cocoa powder
2 egg whites
1 TBSP vanilla extract
1 tsp baking powder
1/4 cup chopped pistachios + 2 TBSP for topping

Preheat the oven to 350⁰ F. Grind the oats into a flour. Then add the remaining ingredients except for the pistachios and blend again. Once blended, stir in ¼ cup chopped pistachios. Spray a cupcake tray with nonstick spray and pour your batter into 5 cupcake molds. Use the other 2 TBSP chopped pistachios to sprinkle on top of the muffins. Bake at 350⁰ F for 30 minutes. Remove and let cool for 10 minutes, then enjoy.

serves 5

nutritional information per serving
173 calories; 11 g fat, 15 g carbs (5 g fiber), 9 g protein

dairy free, gluten free

"many people strive for success in order to find happiness when, in fact, the inverse is true. strive for happiness and you shall find success.

Dr. Steve Maraboli

miscellaneous

This chapter is anything and everything in between. Sometimes the traditional dessert options just aren't what's needed to do the trick. You need options to find that sweet tooth satisfaction.

Red Velvet Protein Bark

3 scoops chocolate whey protein powder
1/2 TBSP dried beet powder (optional)
1/2 cup coconut flour
1/4 cup almond meal/flour (or more coconut flour)
1/4 cup baking stevia
1/4 cup coconut butter
1/4 cup unsweetened applesauce
3/4 cup unsweetened almond milk
1 tsp vanilla extract
5-7 drops red food coloring (optional)
10 oz sugar free white chocolate

In a large bowl, mix all of the ingredients except for the chocolate. The beet powder is optional, but it gives it the sweet 'red velvet' taste. Line a 9x9 dish with cling wrap. Melt 5 oz of sugar free white chocolate onto the base of the dish. Place the dish in the refrigerator for 30 minutes to solidify the chocolate, then spread the red velvet batter on top. Melt the remaining 5 oz of chocolate on top of the red velvet batter; place in the fridge for 30-45 minutes to solidify the chocolate. Then cut into 9 even pieces and enjoy. Store any extras in the refrigerator.

If dairy free, some type of protein powder is required. Use a plant-based protein powder (no milk) instead of whey protein. Use dark chocolate (no milk) instead of white chocolate. This would also make the recipe vegan.

serves 9

nutritional information per serving
293 calories; 20 g fat, 20 g carbs (3 g fiber), 12 g protein

dairy free friendly, gluten free, vegan friendly

Carrot Cake Bread

1 cup raw oats
1/2 cup almond meal/four
2 scoops vanilla whey protein powder
1/3 cup chopped walnuts (or pecans)
1/4 cup baking stevia
1 TBSP baking powder
1/2 tsp baking soda
1 TBSP cinnamon
1 tsp nutmeg
1 tsp ginger
3/4 cup pureed carrots (6 oz)
1 whole egg
2 egg whites
1/2 tsp vanilla extract
1/4 cup unsweetened almond milk

Preheat the oven to 350° F. Grind the oats into a flour. Then add it to all of the remaining ingredients in a bowl. For the pureed carrots, it is easiest to purchase baby food; it is pure carrot puree. Mix everything evenly. Spray a bread loaf pan with nonstick spray and pour the batter in. Bake at 350° F for 25-27 minutes. Let cool for 10-15 minutes, then cut into 12 slices. Enjoy.

If dairy free, omit the whey protein entirely.

serves 12

nutritional information per serving
110 calories; 6 g fat, 8 g carbs (2 g fiber), 8 g protein

dairy free friendly, gluten free

Samoa Cookie Bars

Base
1 cup raw oats
1 cup almond meal/flour
2 TBSP coconut oil
1/2 cup unsweetened applesauce
2 stevia packets

Topping
1 cup pitted dates (160 g)
1.5 cups unsweetened almond milk
2 tsp vanilla extract
2/3 cup unsweetened coconut

Chocolate Drizzle
2 TBSP unsweetened cocoa powder
2 TBSP water
3 stevia packets

Preheat the oven to 350⁰ F. Grind the oats into a flour. In a bowl, mix the oats with the remaining base ingredients. Spray a 4x9 baking dish with nonstick spray and spread the base dough into the dish. Bake at 350⁰ F for 18-20 minutes. Prepare the topping. Blend the dates in a blender into fine pieces. If the dates are not soft enough, it helps to let them soak in water for at least 3 hours. Place the chopped dates in a small pan over a stove with the almond milk and vanilla extract. Let simmer over a low heat, stirring often to prevent burning. Once the sauce has thickened like caramel, stir in the coconut. Spread this topping on top of the cookie base once it has finished baking. Mix the cocoa powder, water, and stevia. Drizzle on top of the bars. Cut into 8 pieces and enjoy.

serves 8

nutritional information per serving
274 calories; 17 g fat, 30 g carbs (6 g fiber), 6 g protein

dairy free, gluten free, vegan

Chocolate Peanut Butter Single Serve Cake

Cake Batter
1 scoop chocolate whey protein powder
2 TBSP coconut flour
2 tsp unsweetened cocoa power
1 egg white
1/4 cup canned pumpkin puree
¼ cup unsweetened almond milk
2 stevia packets
1/2 tsp baking powder

Peanut Butter Swirl
2 TBSP peanut flour
1.5 TBSP water

Preheat the oven to 350° F. Mix all of the cake batter ingredients in a bowl. Spray a ramekin with non-stick spray and pour the chocolate cake batter in. Mix the peanut flour and water to make the peanut butter swirl. Add it on top of the chocolate batter and swirl. Bake at 350° F for 25-28 minutes. Let cool for 5 minutes and then enjoy.

If dairy free, omit the whey protein entirely.

serves 1

nutritional information per serving
291 calories; 6 g fat, 24 g carbs (11 g fiber), 40 g protein

dairy free friendly, gluten free

Peach Almond Biscottis

1/2 cup raw oats
1/2 cup spelt flour
1 whole egg
1 egg white
1 tsp coconut oil
3 TBSP chopped almonds
1 tsp baking powder
1/8 tsp baking soda
1/4 cup baking stevia
1/4 fresh peach, chopped (50 g)

Preheat the oven to 350⁰ F. Grind the oats into a flour. Then add it to the remaining ingredients in a bowl and mix evenly. The batter should be pretty thick and hold its form. Line a baking sheet with parchment paper. Spoon the biscotti batter onto the parchment paper, spreading out evenly but not too thin – approximately 1.5 inches thick. Bake at 350⁰ F for 20 minutes. Remove the pan from the oven and slice the biscottis into 8 pieces. Flip them on their sides and bake at 275⁰ F for 15 minutes, or until lightly browned. Flip each biscotti onto its other side, then bake another 15 minutes at 275⁰ F. Enjoy.

If gluten free, buckwheat flour can be used instead of spelt flour.

serves 8

nutritional information per serving
82 calories; 3 g fat, 10 g carbs (2 g fiber), 3 g protein

dairy free, gluten free friendly

Pumpkin Swirl Protein Cheesecake

Crust
1.5 cups almond meal/flour
1 TBSP coconut oil
1 TBSP almond butter
2 TBSP sugar free syrup

Cheesecake
2, 6 oz containers of plain greek yogurt
8 oz container of 1/3 fat cream cheese
2 whole eggs
2 egg whites
2 scoops vanilla whey protein powder
1.5 cups baking stevia

Pumpkin Pie Swirl
1/2 cup canned pumpkin
1/2 tsp pumpkin pie spice
1/3 cup unsweetened almond milk
1/4 cup baking stevia

Preheat the oven to 350^{0} F. Mix all of the crust ingredients in a bowl. Press firmly into the base of a pie pan. The crust should bind together as you press it into the pan. Then, blend all of the cheesecake ingredients in a blender or food processor. Pour over the cheesecake crust. Finally, mix all of the pumpkin swirl ingredients in a bowl. Dollop on top of the cheesecake and swirl with a knife. Bake the cheesecake at 350^{0} F for 60 minutes. Let cool at room temperature for 30 minutes, then refrigerate for 4 hours or longer before serving. Cut into 8 slices and enjoy.

serves 8

nutritional information per serving
288 calories; 20 g fat, 12 g carbs (3 g fiber), 20 g protein

gluten free

Apple Pie Toaster Strudels

1 medium apple (200 g)
1/2 cup water
1/2 tsp cinnamon
1/8 tsp ginger
1/4 tsp vanilla extract
3 stevia packets
6 egg roll wrappers
1/2 TBSP coconut oil
cinnamon & stevia (for topping)

Peel and dice the apple. Combine in a pot or pan with the water, cinnamon, ginger, vanilla, and stevia packets. Let the mixture simmer on the stove for 6-7 minutes, until the apples are soft. Drain the apples to remove any excess water. Lay the egg roll wrappers on a flat surface, placing 2 TBSP of the cooked apple mixture inside each one. Wrap tightly, placing each on a sprayed baking sheet. Brush the top of each roll with coconut oil; you will only need ½ TBSP coconut oil total. This allows for the wraps to crisp in the oven. Then dust the tops with more cinnamon and stevia. Bake at 350° F for 13-15 minutes until the tops are lightly browned. Remove and enjoy warm.

serves 6

nutritional information per serving
88 calories; 2 g fat, 17 g carbs (1 g fiber), 2 g protein

dairy free

Carrot Cake Truffles

1 scoop vanilla whey protein powder
2 TBSP coconut flour
2 TBSP almond butter
1/4 cup pureed carrots (2 oz)
1/8 tsp cinnamon
1/8 tsp ginger
pinch of nutmeg
1 stevia packet
2 oz sugar free white chocolate

In a bowl, mix all of the ingredients except for the white chocolate. For the pureed carrots, it is easiest to purchase baby food; it is pure carrot puree. Once evenly mixed, it should be very thick and difficult to stir. Place in the fridge for 1 hour to thicken more. Microwave the white chocolate for 30 seconds at a time until just barely melted. Using your hands, mold the carrot cake batter into 6 balls, dipping each ball into the melted chocolate. Coat the truffles entirely. Place them back in the fridge for 30 minutes to solidify the chocolate, then enjoy.

If dairy free, some type of protein powder is required. Use a plant-based protein powder (no milk) instead of whey protein. Use dark chocolate (no milk) instead of white chocolate. This would also make the recipe vegan.

serves 6

nutritional information per serving
111 calories; 7 g fat, 8 g carbs (2 g fiber), 6 g protein

dairy free friendly, gluten free, vegan friendly

Coconut Almond Donuts

Donuts
1/3 cup raw oats
1 TBSP almond flour/meal
1/2 scoop vanilla whey protein powder
3 egg whites
1/4 tsp almond extract
1/2 tsp baking powder
1 stevia packet

Icing
1 TBSP coconut oil
1 TBSP vanilla whey protein powder

Topping
1 TBSP sliced almonds

Preheat the oven to 350° F. In a blender, grind the oats into a flour. Then add the remaining donut ingredients and blend again. Spray a donut pan with nonstick spray and pour the batter into 4 of the molds. Bake at 350° F for 10 minutes. Remove and let cool. While cooling, make the icing by mixing the coconut oil and protein powder. Once the donuts are fully cooled, drizzle the icing on top and sprinkle the slivered almonds. Enjoy.

If dairy free, omit the whey protein entirely.

serves 4

nutritional information per serving
110 calories; 6 g fat, 6 g carbs (1 g fiber), 11 g protein

dairy free friendly, gluten free

Peanut Butter Crunch Brownies

1/2 cup raw oats
1/2 cup chocolate whey protein powder (60 g)
1/2 cup unsweetened cocoa powder
1/2 cup peanut flour
1/2 cup peanut butter
1/4 cup baking stevia
1 tsp baking powder
1 cup unsweetened almond milk
1/4 cup chopped peanuts, for topping

Preheat the oven to 350° F. Grind the oats into a flour. In a bowl, mix the remaining ingredients with the ground oats (except for the peanuts) until even. The batter should be really thick and chocolatey. Spray an 8x8 dish with nonstick spray and pour the batter in. Sprinkle the top with chopped peanuts. Bake at 350° F for 20 minutes. Let cool 10 minutes, cut into 9 pieces, and enjoy.

If dairy free, some protein powder is required. Use a plant-based protein powder (no milk) instead of whey protein. This would also make the recipe vegan.

serves 9

nutritional information per serving
191 calories; 11 g fat, 12 g carbs (5 g fiber), 14 g protein

dairy free friendly, gluten free, vegan friendly

"finish every day and be done with it. you have done what you could; some blunders and absurdities no doubt crept in; forget them as soon as you can. tomorrow is a new day; you shall begin it serenely and with too high a spirit to be encumbered with your old nonsense."

Ralph Waldo Emerson

Made in the USA
Middletown, DE
27 January 2016